"TO MY CHEERLEADERS... SARAH, BETHANY, STACY."

—D.B.M.

Tiny Tern Takes Flight
Hardcover first edition • November 2024 • ISBN: 978-1-958629-55-0
Paperback first edition • May 2025 • ISBN: 978-1-958629-83-3
eBook first edition • November 2024 • ISBN: 978-1-958629-56-7

Written by Donna B. McKinney, Text © 2024
Illustrated by Fiona Osbaldstone, Illustrations © 2024

Project Manager, Cover and Book Design: Caitlin Burnham
Editors: Marlee Brooks and Hannah Thelen
Editorial Assistants: Shannon Dinniman, Carmina López, Charlotte Shao, and Susan Stark

Available in Spanish as Charrancito se lanza a volar
    Spanish paperback first edition • May 2025 • ISBN: 978-1-958629-81-9
    Spanish eBook first edition • May 2025 • ISBN: 978-1-958629-82-6

Teacher's Guide available at the Educational Resources page of ScienceNaturally.com.

Published by:
    Science, Naturally! – An imprint of Platypus Media, LLC
    750 First Street NE, Suite 700
    Washington, DC 20002
    202-465-4798
    Info@ScienceNaturally.com • ScienceNaturally.com

Distributed to the book trade by:
    Baker & Taylor Publisher Services (North America)
    Toll-free: (888) 814 0208
    orders@btpubservices.com • Btpubservices.com

Library of Congress Control Number: 2024937201

10 9 8 7 6 5 4 3 2 1

Schools, libraries, government and non-profit organizations can receive a bulk discount for quantity orders. Contact us at the address above or email us at Info@ScienceNaturally.com.

The front cover may be reproduced freely, without modification, for review or non-commercial educational purposes.

All rights reserved. No part of this book may be reproduced in any form without the express written permission of the publisher. Front cover exempted (see above).

Printed in China.

Tiny Tern Takes Flight

BY DONNA B. McKINNEY

ILLUSTRATED BY FIONA OSBALDSTONE

Science, Naturally!
An imprint of Platypus Media, LLC
Washington, D.C.

Arctic Terns live in shivering cold lands near the North Pole.

Each summer day Tiny Tern, a small but mighty bird, joins other terns in the hunt for food.

SWOOSH!

Catching flying insects buzzing through the warm air.

Diving into icy waters for edible ocean critters.

SPLASH!

Scooping out a nest on the rough, rocky ground of open tundra.

SCRITCH-SCRATCH!

Now eggs are in the nests.

Tiny, pale, olive-colored eggs with splashes of black and brown.

Chicks hatch.
They hide. They grow.
They fly.
The tern colony brims
with boisterous bird sounds on summer days.

KREE-ERRR!

KREE-ERRR!

Terns protect eggs and chicks against fierce predators great and small.
Danger is near.
Fox, polar bear, and gull.
A mink slinks toward the nest on quiet feet,
looking to steal an egg.

WHIZZ! ZIP!

Fearless terns dive bomb the mink.
The mink scampers, no match for brave terns.
Tiny, pale, olive-colored eggs with splashes
of black and brown are safe.

Summer's end draws near.

Daylight hours grow short.

Cold air blows. Sunrise, sunset.

Day by day, sunlight creeps toward darkness,
as Earth turns on its axis.
Slowly, surely, summer sunshine fades.

One day, a sudden hush blankets the tundra.

Shhhhhhh...

Terns everywhere, but not a sound.

In silence, they ready themselves for flight.

A rush of flapping wings.

SWOOSH! SWIRL! SWISH!

Tiny Tern soars like an acrobat in the air.

Swiftly the flock lifts from the tundra,
a churning cloud rising skyward.
TWIRL! TWIRL! TWIRL!
Terns, young and old, fill the air.

Their journey southward begins.
Behind them, sunlight falters and fades as winter falls.
All is shivering, icy-cold, dark, frozen.

Ahead lies warmth and summer light.
Flocks of terns fly toward brighter days,
chasing sunlight
from the North Pole to the South Pole.
Ordinary Tiny Tern's extraordinary journey has begun.
The flight is long,
Tiny Tern must not delay.

Terns eat while flying.
Terns even sleep while gliding,
soaring above ocean waters.

RISE!

GLIDE!

ZOOM!

Riding thermal air currents. Rising on updrafts. Feeling the wind lift and carry their slender bodies higher, further, southward toward summer sunshine.

Days slip away.

Weeks pass.

Ocean beneath, sky above, terns sail the winds.

Lakes, hills, farms form a patchwork on the ground below.
Tiny Tern soars
till shivering Arctic cold and darkness is far behind.

But what's that dark rumbling ahead?
Gathering clouds in the distance—
a storm approaches!
Gusting winds push against Tiny Tern's small body.
Will Tiny Tern be lost in the swirl of wind and rain?

The storm shoves Tiny Tern off course.
WHOOSH!
Where is the flock?

Tiny Tern keeps flying, soaring toward sunshine.
Pressing through the storm.

Like fluttering kites, the flock fills the skies.
Tiny Tern glides again on calm breezes,
carried by the wind.

Finally!
The long journey ends.

There's safety in the Antarctic sunlight.
Ahhhh...
Warmth, food, endless days of light.
Tiny Tern finds rest.
Tiny Tern plays on sunlit breezes.

The Antarctic brims with boisterous bird sounds all summer. Floating on icebergs, terns nap in endless sunshine.

KREE-ERRR!

KREE-ERRR!

KREE-ERRR!

WHIZZ!

Terns dive for the bounty ocean waters offer.

SWOOSH!

Tiny Tern gathers strength.

Because slowly, surely, summer sunlight fades in this place.

Sunrise, sunset, day by day.

Sunlight creeps toward darkness,

as Earth turns on its axis.

Antarctic summer days grow shorter.

In the far north, Arctic winter cold eases.

Sunshine returns.

Soon the flock rises and soars. *TWIRL!*
A quivering cloud of birds against the sky.
Terns look to the north, searching again for summer sunlight. *SOAR!*

The journey is long the other way, too.
Tiny Tern must not delay.
Ahead are long nights,
fierce winds,
dangerous storms.

But Tiny Tern does not turn from danger.
High above, Tiny Tern follows summer days,
chasing sunlight
from pole to pole.
Tiny Tern's journey homeward begins.

From the South Pole to the North Pole,
from the Antarctic to the Arctic,
terns fly.

Year after year,
journey upon journey,
Terns fly from the North Pole to the South Pole and back again.

Ordinary terns make extraordinary flights,
living in two summers every year,
seeing more daylight than any other animal on land or sea.
Tiny Tern touches the tips of the Earth.

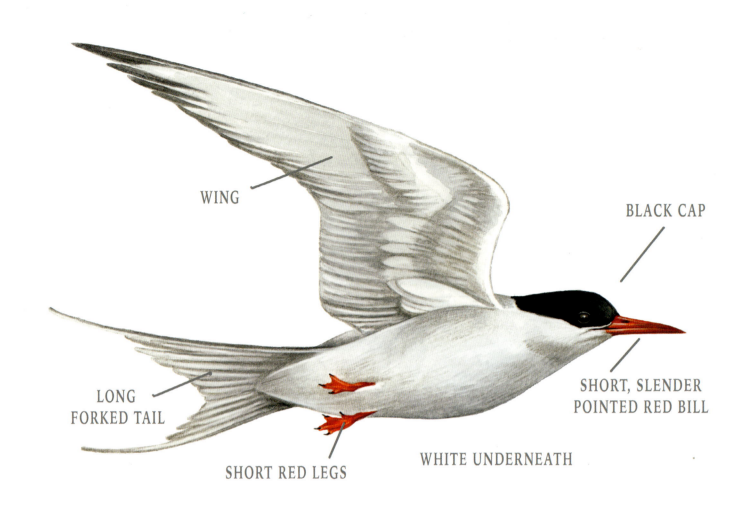

TAIL FEATHER SIZES

WING FEATHER SIZES

LEARN MORE ABOUT ARCTIC TERNS

The Arctic Tern is quite the ordinary seabird. It eats ordinary food like tiny fish and insects. It builds its nests in ordinary places, like the rocky ground near water. The tern's feathers are gray-white with a jet-black feather cap atop its head. Its beak and webbed feet are a tomato-red color. The tern weighs around 4 ounces, or 125 grams, which is about as light as a deck of playing cards or a baseball. Tiny Tern is a young Arctic Tern. Unlike the adults, young terns have more gray on their bodies and less black on their heads. Their beaks are dark-colored, not tomato red like the mature adults.

Every year, ordinary terns make an extraordinary journey, flying from the North Pole to the South Pole and back again. Scientists who track Arctic Terns believe that their trip from the high Arctic region to the Southern Ocean around Antarctica may be the longest migration of any animal. Scientists have fitted terns with tiny tracking devices that record their travels. Terns can fly as fast as 25 miles (40 kilometers) per hour. Some terns fly about 50,000 miles each year, or 80,000 kilometers.

TERNS IN THE ARCTIC

When it is summer in the northern hemisphere—June, July, August—terns live in the Arctic region, near the North Pole. Here they build nests on the rocky open tundra, on small islands, or even on floating ice. During the long summer days, the chicks hatch and grow, making their first flights when they are around 24 days old.

The terns dive into cold ocean waters to catch their food—small fish, shrimp, marine worms. They also catch and eat insects that fly through the air. Sometimes they find and eat berries growing on land.

Foxes, gulls, polar bears, and seals are just some of the predators who might attack the terns. When they are threatened, a flock of terns will dive bomb the predators to scare them away. The fearless Arctic Tern is not afraid to attack a polar bear that is threatening its nest.

When summer is ending in the Arctic, the tern colony prepares to migrate south. Suddenly one day, all the noisy bird calls grow silent. This tern behavior is called a "dread." Following the silence, the colony takes flight all at once, headed toward the South Pole.

MIGRATION

The terns do not fly in a straight line southward. They tend to follow a wandering path, searching for food, avoiding bad storms, and flying near land. They can glide for long distances, even sleeping while in flight. This migration takes several months.

Terns are built for long flight. Their short, stubby legs make them clumsy when walking on land. But in the air, they use their tail feathers—spread wide

or pulled together tight—to allow them to glide, hover, and dive. Their hollow bones make them extra lightweight.

The long migration is challenging. But staying in the Arctic region through the winter months, with its harsh cold and dark days, would be even more dangerous. For the terns, the long migration is their survival superpower.

TERNS IN THE ANTARCTIC

The terns arrive in the Antarctic region in November as summer has just begun. They spend their days floating on icebergs, hunting for food, and soaking up the endless sunshine.

As the Antarctic summer comes to an end in early March, the terns begin their migration home to the Arctic lands. The tail winds are favorable for the flight home. Terns arrive back in the Arctic region at the end of May as summer and endless daylight begins.

CHASING THE SUN

These summer months in the Arctic and Antarctic regions provide almost 24 hours of daylight. This sunlight makes it easier for terns to see their food. Summer weather also generally means calmer weather, so flying is easier. Through their migration, Arctic Terns follow the summer sun all year long. Some scientists suggest that terns see more sunlight throughout their 30-year lifespan than any other animal.

ABOUT THE AUTHOR AND ILLUSTRATOR

DONNA B. McKINNEY is the author of over 20 children's books, including her most recent release *Lights On!*. Before she was writing books for kids, Donna worked at the U.S. Naval Research Laboratory in Washington, D.C., writing about the science behind their research into space satellites, robots, and more. She now lives in North Carolina with her two full-of-mischief dogs. When she's not writing, she enjoys hiking, fishing, and playing pickleball. She can be reached at Donna.McKinney@ScienceNaturally.com.

Born in Kent, England, **FIONA OSBALDSTONE** loved painting as a kid and used to paint her own versions of fictional characters. She always wanted to do something with art and attended the Kent Institute of Art & Design. She was inspired by the works of David Shepherd and Norman Rockwell for their detail and diversely different styles. Her work includes natural history, botanicals, people, and scenes. Outside of the artistic field, although not too far removed, she loves pottery, photography, and cycling.